D1305787

Covington, Ohio 45619

EXAMINING DISASTERS

EXAMINING PANDEMICS

BY NINA ROLFES

CLARA
HOUSE
BOOKS

J.R. Clarke Public Library
102 E. Spring St
Covington, Ohio 45318

First published in 2015 by Clara House Books, an imprint of
The Oliver Press, Inc.

Copyright © 2015 CBM LLC

Clara House Books
5707 West 36th Street
Minneapolis, MN 55416
USA

Editors: Mirella Miller and Arnold Ringstad
Series Designer: Maggie Villaume

All rights reserved.

Picture Credits
Hinochika/Shutterstock Images, cover, 1; Cynthia Goldsmith/CDC, 4; James Gathany/CDC,
7; Andreas Rentz/Getty Images/Thinkstock, 8; U.S. Army, 10; Sandy Huffaker/Getty Images/
Thinkstock, 12; CDC, 14, 40; Christopher Furlong/Getty Images/Thinkstock, 16; Joe Raedle/
Getty Images/Thinkstock, 18–19; Brendan Smialowski/Getty Images/Thinkstock; 21; Dr. Arthur
Siegelman/Visuals Unlimited/Corbis, 22; MAPS.com/Corbis, 25; Bettmann/Corbis, 27; Chung
Sung-Jun/Getty Images/Thinkstock, 28; Peter Macdiarmid/Press Association/AP Images, 30;
Edward A. "Doc" Rogers, 33; Cade Martin/CDC, 34; Natalie Behring-Chisholm/Getty Images/
Thinkstock, 36; David Goldman/AP Images, 39; Michael Duff/AP Images, 42

Every attempt has been made to clear copyright. Should there be any inadvertent omission,
please apply to the publisher for rectification.

Library of Congress Cataloging-in-Publication Data

Rolfes, Nina, author.
  Examining pandemics / by Nina Rolfes.
     pages cm. – (Examining disasters)
  Audience: Grades 7-8.
  Includes bibliographical references and index.
  ISBN 978-1-934545-66-9 (hardcover : alk. paper) – ISBN 978-1-934545-82-9 (ebook)
  1. Epidemics–Juvenile literature. 2. Communicable diseases–Juvenile literature. I. Title.

  RA653.5.R65 2015
  614.4'9–dc23

                                    2014044475

Printed in the United States of America
CG1022015

www.oliverpress.com

CONTENTS

ONE

INFLUENZA PANDEMIC

A terrible disaster struck the world in 2009 and 2010. In the course of about 15 months, approximately 60.8 million people in the United States became sick. A strain of influenza, or flu, called H1N1 was spreading quickly. This was the first major influenza pandemic, or large outbreak, of the 2000s. Some estimate as many as 284,500 to 575,400 people worldwide died. Determining the number of people affected is difficult. Some of the hardest-hit countries, especially in Africa, often do not record medical statistics or deaths from specific illnesses. Numbers from these countries are only estimates.

The 2009 H1N1 virus quickly spread from person to person.

5

A CDC microbiologist examines an influenza virus to understand the infection better.

THE PANDEMIC SEVERITY INDEX

In 2007, the U.S. Department of Health and Human Services recommended a system to categorize pandemics on a scale of 1 to 5, with 5 being the worst. The scale, called the Pandemic Severity Index, calls for different responses based on the level. These responses range from simple measures, such as washing hands for low-level pandemics, to more drastic steps, such as closing schools and businesses for more serious pandemics. The severity of a pandemic is based on how fast the virus is spread from person to person, as well as the number of people who die from the disease.

The name H1N1 refers to the proteins hemagglutinin (H) and neuraminidase (N) in the virus. The number refers to the protein's subtype. There are sixteen subtypes of hemagglutinin, and nine subtypes of neuraminidase. H1N1 was first detected in a boy in Mexico in February 2009. The first U.S. case of H1N1 was diagnosed on April 15, 2009.

The Centers for Disease Control and Prevention (CDC) is the government agency responsible for protecting the United States from health, safety, and security threats. The CDC defines an epidemic as many cases of a disease in any given area. If that disease spreads to a wider area, covering multiple countries or continents, it is considered a pandemic.

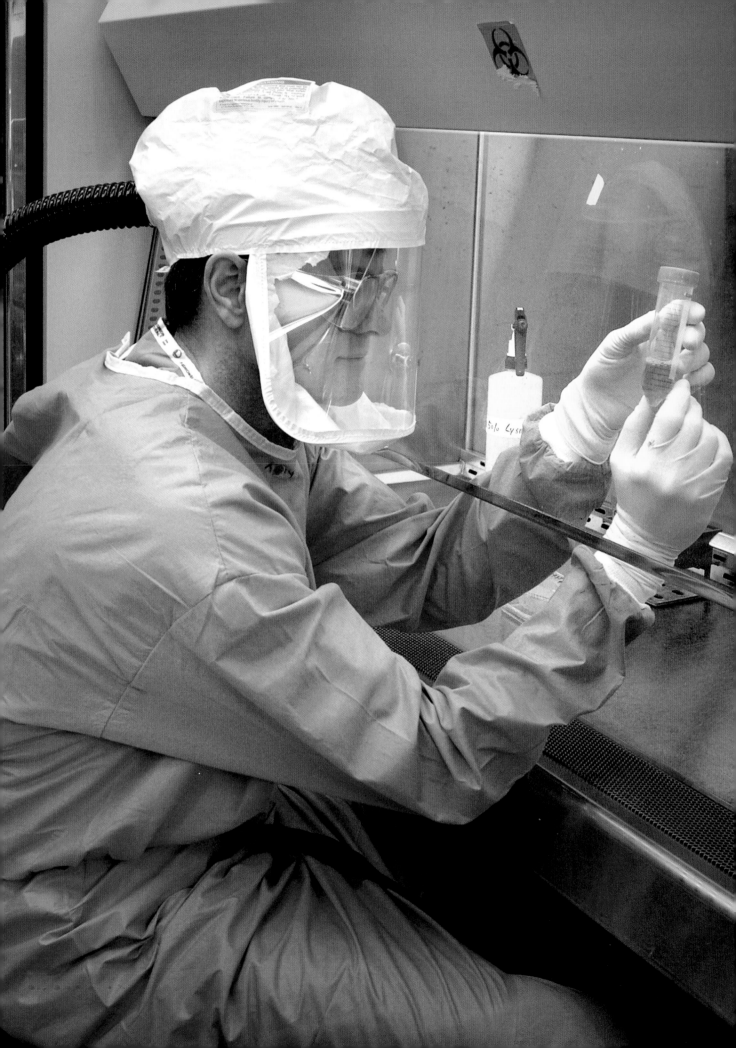

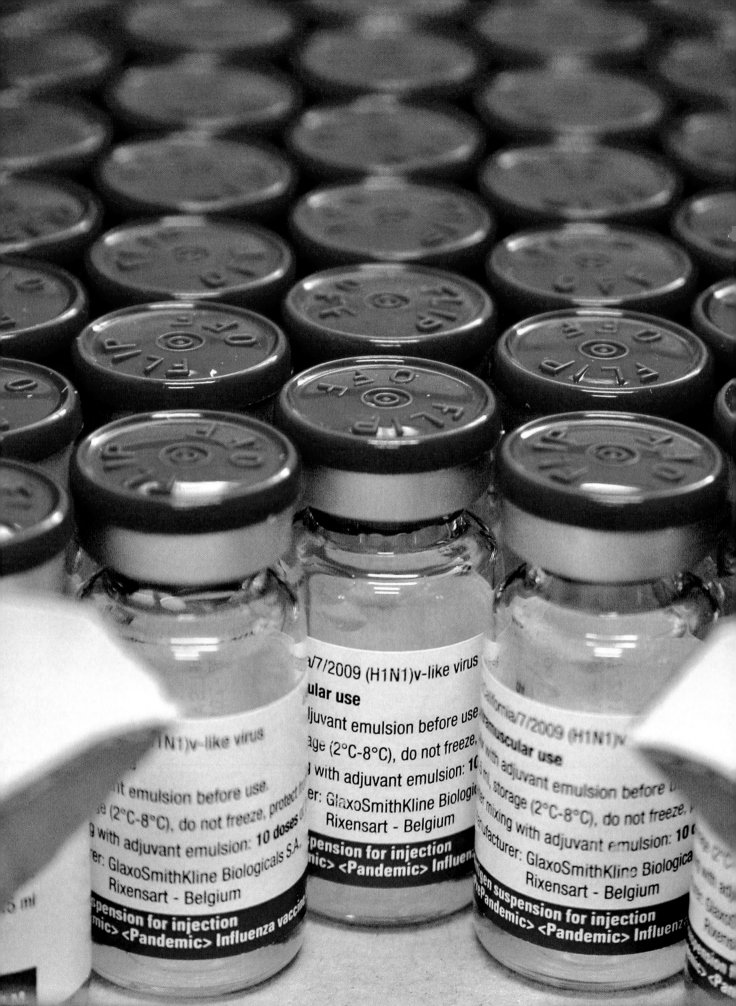

The H1N1 vaccine was sent around the world to be distributed to the most vulnerable populations first.

In June 2009, the World Health Organization (WHO) declared H1N1 a pandemic.

The CDC quickly started developing a vaccine that would protect people from H1N1. Vaccines are weakened versions of a virus that are injected into people to train their bodies to fight off the disease. Within two months of the first official diagnosis, there were more than 18,000 confirmed cases of H1N1 in the United States. Eventually, people living in 74 countries got the disease. Supplies of the vaccine were low, so it was first given to the most vulnerable populations, including the elderly and those with other medical conditions.

SIX PHASES OF A PANDEMIC

The World Health Organization (WHO) has divided the life of a pandemic into six phases. In phase one, viruses in animals do not cause disease in humans. In phase two, a virus among animals causes infection in humans, and therefore the possibility of a pandemic exists. In phase three, small groups of humans are infected. In phase four, the disease is spread through enough human-to-human contact to cause greater outbreaks. In phase five, the virus spreads between two countries. An outbreak is upgraded to phase six when the virus spreads to more than two countries.

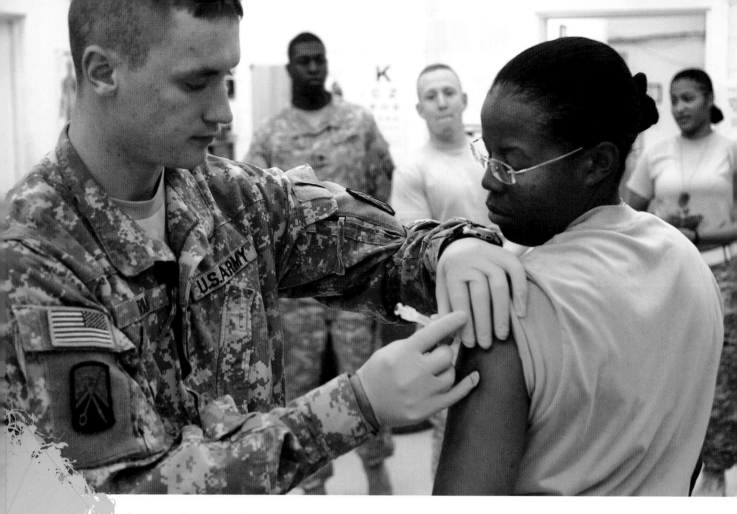

Members of the U.S. Army receive the seasonal influenza vaccine.

END OF THE PANDEMIC

In November 2009 the disease slowed down, allowing nearly 80 million people to get doses of the quickly produced vaccine. A large vaccinated population helped stop H1N1 from spreading as quickly. On August 10, 2010, the WHO declared the H1N1 pandemic was over.

However, influenza is a disease that returns on a regular basis. The flu is more common during the winter months, peaking in the Northern Hemisphere in February. The time of year when influenza is most common and widespread is called the flu season. Although it stopped rapidly spreading, H1N1 did not disappear. In fact, H1N1 has returned every flu season since, along with the regular seasonal influenza. Now an H1N1 vaccination is included in the same dose as the seasonal flu shot. People are being protected against both diseases with one vaccine.

The flu is not the only virus that can cause fear. Many pandemics have surfaced over the years. Some are quickly cured, while others take longer to contain. The Ebola outbreak in 2014 was the most recent virus to spread.

HOW SCIENCE WORKS
SWINE FLU MISCONCEPTIONS

H1N1 was nicknamed swine flu because it was originally found in pigs. Members of the media were quick to use the name "swine flu" for the virus that caused the pandemic of 2009, because the name was catchier and easier to remember than H1N1. This name led people to believe mistakenly they could catch the disease from eating pig products. Several countries banned pork product imports. Scientists had to explain how the virus worked, and that it could only be transmitted from human to human. Scientists pointed to evidence gathered over many years that showed how diseases spread. They pushed for the disease to be referred to as H1N1 rather than swine flu. The public relations effort succeeded in getting many media outlets to refer to the disease as H1N1, but the name swine flu was still used by the general public.

TWO

TOO CLOSE FOR COMFORT

Contagious diseases spread from one human to another when there is close contact between them. Some viruses can easily move through the air from one person to another. Touching people who are ill, or touching something they touched, can also spread certain diseases. Disease microbes can live for 48 hours or more outside a person. If an infected person touches a doorknob, someone who touches it hours later may become infected.

Masks are an effective way to prevent the spread of disease microbes. A single sneeze can send tiny microbes across a room. These can infect anyone who comes into contact with them. Unless a mask

Some people living in Mexico chose to wear masks to block out microbes after the H1N1 outbreak.

OCTOBER

NOVEMBER

DECEMBER

JANUARY

■ No Report   ■ Sporadic   ■ Regional
■ No Activity   ■ Local   ■ Widespread

THE SPREAD OF INFLUENZA

These maps show the spread of influenza in the United States between October 2013 and January 2014. It was not a pandemic, but the maps show how fast diseases can spread. Do you notice any patterns? What happens to the rate of influenza in colder areas? What happens to islands?

blocks them, microbes can easily invade people's bodies through the nose or mouth.

VECTORS

People also can become infected with viruses by living close to vectors. A vector is a living thing that spreads a disease to another living thing. Mosquitoes are vectors for some of the most contagious diseases in the world. They have contributed to malaria pandemics. In human communities, people usually collect and store water, creating an environment perfect for mosquito growth. Mosquitoes hatch their eggs in standing water. Adult mosquitoes bite animals and people to access their blood for food. In the process, mosquitoes transfer parasites to the creatures they bite, and this is how they spread diseases.

Stored food can also be exposed to disease. Rats and mice, as well as their fleas, can host many diseases. Hantavirus is one deadly disease spread by contact with infected rats and mice. Cows, sheep, pigs, chickens, and other domestic animals can also carry infectious diseases.

When an infection jumps from an animal to a human, it is called a zoonotic disease. More than half of the 1,700 known viruses, bacteria,

NATURAL RESERVOIRS

The host or carrier of a contagious disease is called a natural reservoir. Mosquitoes are a natural reservoir for malaria. Scientists try to determine the natural reservoirs of the viruses they discover, because this helps them learn more about the life cycle of the disease and how it spreads. Then they can work on ways to control the disease.

Pigs are just one of the domestic animals that carry diseases that can spread to humans.

and other microbes that infect people are zoonotic diseases.

POOR SANITATION

Poor sanitation can also increase the spread of disease. Water contaminated with waste can carry diseases such as cholera, dysentery, and typhoid fever. If human waste is stored in unsanitary conditions, such as in open sewers, disease can spread. The flies that live near waste can also be vectors of infectious diseases, passing them on to other organisms. Human travel is one of the fastest and easiest ways for a disease to spread. When people travel to a new place, they are exposed to new microbes. People also bring unfamiliar microbes to the places they visit. An epidemic can start when a new disease is introduced to a population of people. Even one person can potentially start a pandemic.

NATURAL DISASTERS

Natural disasters can also give diseases a chance to spread. When floods, earthquakes, hurricanes, and other natural disasters happen, spreading disease can sometimes take more lives than the original disaster. Broken sewer lines can contaminate clean water systems. New diseases can be carried in from other areas. Natural disasters often lead to shortages of food, clean water, and medical care, leaving people more vulnerable to disease. Diseases spread in war-torn countries for similar

CHOLERA, DYSENTERY, AND TYPHOID FEVER

Poor sanitation leads to the spread of deadly diseases. Cholera is a disease of the small intestine that causes severe diarrhea and decreases bodily fluids. Dysentery also causes diarrhea by inflaming the intestine and causing stomach pain. Typhoid fever causes blood poisoning, headache, fever, and sleeplessness.

People in Haiti are vaccinated against cholera after the 2010 earthquake devastated the country.

reasons. Finally, pandemics can occur because of a lack of good medical care and transportation for ill people.

Most people have a healthy immune system, which works to protect against flu viruses and other germs.

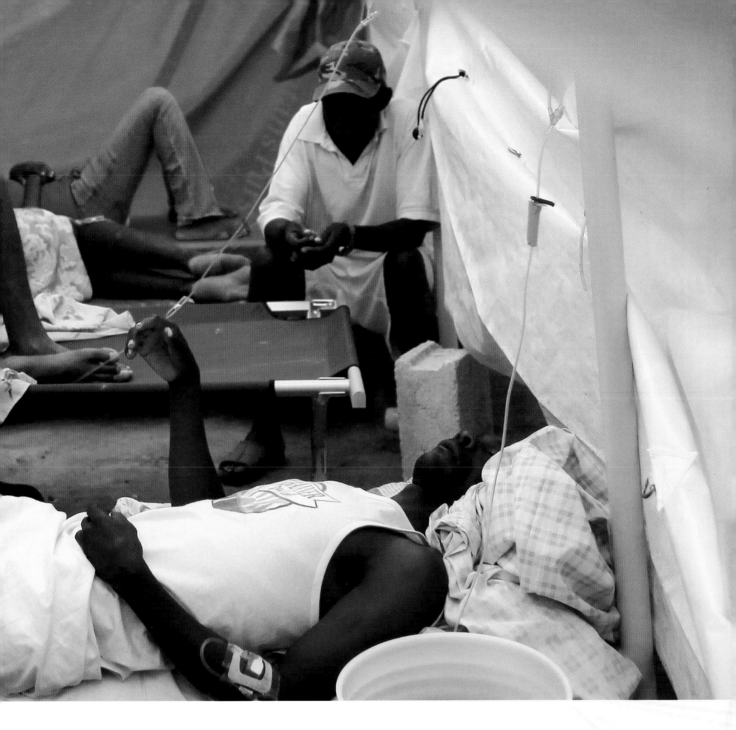

People encounter potentially disease-causing microbes every day, but their immune systems are able to fight them off. However, if the immune system encounters a new and unusual microbe, it may be unable to fight it effectively.

Newborn babies, young people, elderly, and those who are already ill are most likely to catch new microbes.

STUDYING PANDEMICS

Virologists, the scientists who study viruses, and epidemiologists, the scientists who study contagious diseases, work to keep up with newly emerging viruses. There are many flu viruses, and they are changing all the time. People are urged to get a flu shot every year, because vaccines must be constantly updated to fight off the latest flu viruses.

Because vaccines must be created from an existing virus, a new virus can potentially infect millions of people before vaccines are available. Epidemiologists and other scientists work around the clock to track, contain, and prevent the spread of disease.

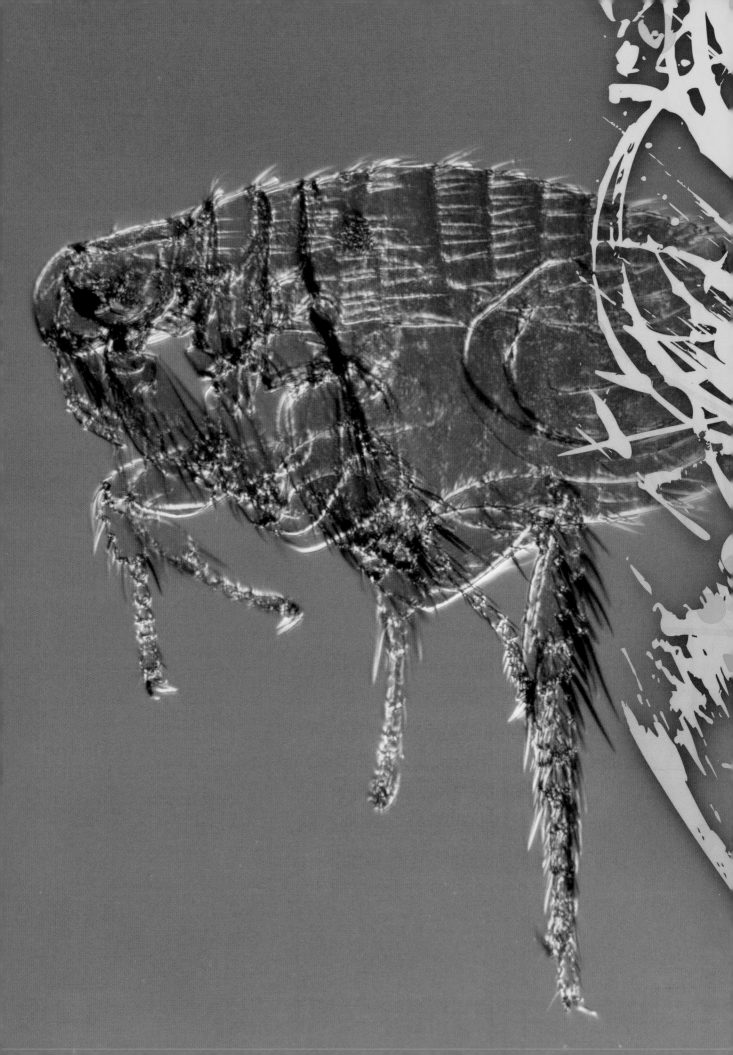

THREE

A HORRIFYING HISTORY

Humans have been subjected to deadly pandemics throughout history. The chances of pandemics happening increased as people formed larger communities, traded with their neighbors, explored new places, and went to war against each other. All of these activities made the spreading of viruses to larger groups of people more likely. Among the first pandemics was the bubonic plague.

By studying genetics, modern scientists discovered the bubonic plague bacteria appeared in China more than 2,600 years ago. Fleas spread the disease by biting rodents that then bit humans.

The oriental rat flea primarily feeds on rats and is the vector of most plague epidemics in Asia, Africa, and South America.

BUBONIC PLAGUE TODAY

The bubonic plague still infects people today, but modern antibiotics can successfully treat the disease. Between 1,000 and 3,000 people contract bubonic plague every year, and approximately 200 of those die because they lack access to treatment. However, the availability of treatment and understanding of how the disease spreads have made it unlikely that bubonic plague will become a full-fledged pandemic again.

Sometime in the 1320s or 1330s, the bubonic plague broke out again in China's Gobi Desert, and this time it spread worldwide. Seagoing Chinese explorers introduced the disease to Europe and later to Africa. The bubonic plague became known as the Black Death. Black, bloody boils the size of apples grew on the victim's skin. Without treatment, approximately half of the people who caught the plague died.

The Black Death swept across Europe in the 1340s. Trading, wars, and unclean conditions in towns and cities helped it spread. Not having medical understanding about the disease also fueled its spread. Some people believed the plague was God's wrath, or anger. They thought they could escape the punishment by leaving their homes, so they left sick family

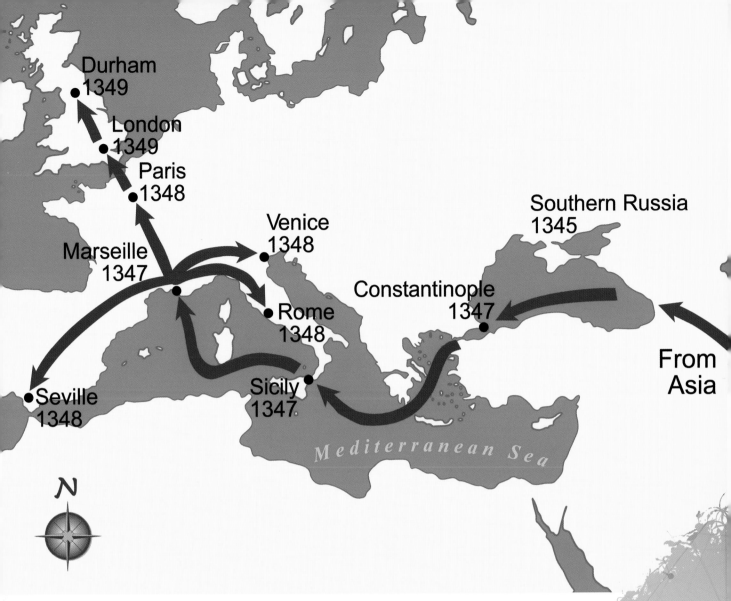

The Black Death swept through Europe in just a few years.

members behind and spread the disease to other areas.
Within five years, the Black Death had killed about one-
third of the European population. It also killed many
people in India and China. The plague had finished
taking its toll by the early 1350s, but it came back several
times over the next few centuries, taking more lives.

SPREADING DISEASE ON PURPOSE

Bioterrorism involves the intentional release of disease-causing materials. Mongol warriors flung plague-infected corpses at their enemies. Europeans gave blankets infected with smallpox to American Indians. In the 1930s, the Japanese army bombed China with plague fleas and infected clothing and supplies. Scientists prepare stockpiles of vaccines against diseases that could be used in bioterrorism today, such as anthrax. In 2001, anthrax was sent through the U.S. Postal Service. Five people were killed, and more than one dozen others were infected.

SMALLPOX

Like the Black Death, smallpox ranks among the most devastating diseases and pandemics in human history. It emerged from northeastern Africa thousands of years ago and began spreading to every populated continent. Smallpox kills about a third of the people it infects. The virus can be passed along through contact.

Smallpox spread throughout Europe, Asia, and Africa in the 1500s. Sea travel and exploration then brought the disease to the rest of the world. It killed millions of American Indians. By the middle of the 1700s, smallpox was present everywhere in the world except for a few islands. During that century, smallpox killed as many as 400,000 people a year.

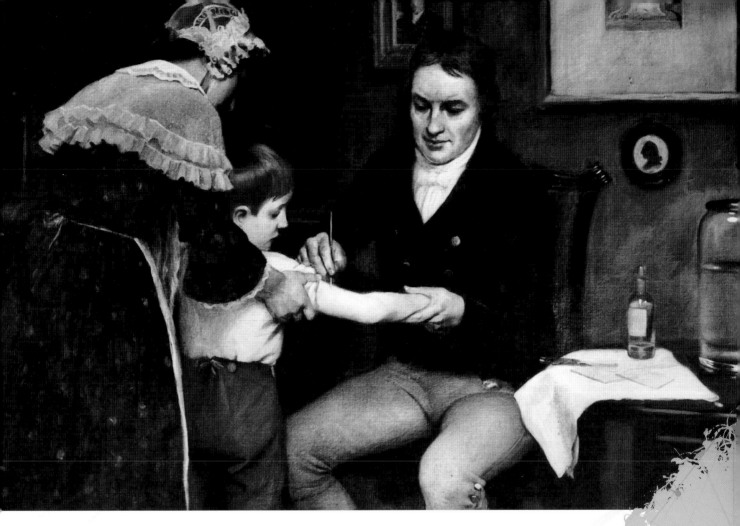

Edward Jenner's work eventually led to the official declaration in 1979 that smallpox had been erased from the planet.

Finally, a vaccine was developed, changing the course of history. In 1796, a scientist named Edward Jenner noticed women who milked cows seemed to be immune to smallpox. He wondered if this was because they were exposed to cowpox, a disease related to smallpox but not as dangerous. To test his theory, Jenner injected cowpox into his gardener's young son and watched what happened. The boy became ill, but he quickly recovered. Then Jenner gave the boy a dose of

Women in a South Korean airport wear masks to help protect against the SARS virus.

smallpox virus, and the boy did not get sick. Jenner had created a vaccine that would eventually wipe out one of the most devastating diseases in human history.

AIDS

The worst pandemic in the last few decades has been acquired immunodeficiency syndrome (AIDS), caused by the human immunodeficiency virus (HIV). AIDS weakens a person's immune system, turning ordinary diseases into fatal illnesses. Since the AIDS pandemic began in the 1980s, it has killed approximately 36 million people.

HOW SCIENCE WORKS
THE SARS VIRUS

In 2002, there was a deadly pandemic known as severe acute respiratory syndrome (SARS). It infected more than 8,000 people and killed more than 700 around the world. Scientists tried to locate the natural reservoir of the mysterious virus. Horseshoe bats in China were discovered to carry a virus related to the SARS virus. Chinese and Australian researchers used a special virus isolation technique and studied the feces of the horseshoe bats. They found the bat virus was 95-percent similar to the SARS virus that infects humans. In 2013, the team confirmed the bat was the host of the virus responsible for the 2002 pandemic. Knowing the origin of the virus can help scientists create a vaccine and better prevention methods for SARS and other potential pandemics.

FOUR

DETECTION AND TRACKING

The first people who broke out with the black boils of bubonic plague had no idea what ailed them until it was too late. But today, scientists have the knowledge and tools to detect, track, contain, manage, and even cure diseases. They are also learning how to prevent these diseases and wipe them out entirely.

For a virus to be identified and tracked, scientists must learn where it came from, where it will go next, and when it will get there. They also need to find out how a disease is transmitted from person to person, during which stages of a disease a person is able to infect others, and how the disease can be effectively treated.

Determining how viruses are related can help scientists predict and prevent pandemics.

1918 TO 1919 INFLUENZA PANDEMIC

A terrible disaster struck the world in 1918 and 1919. In the course of about 18 months, approximately 500 million people around the world became sick with the flu. More than 50 million people died from the worst outbreak of influenza in history. It was made illegal in some public places to cough, spit, or sneeze. People wore masks when they went outside. The disease spread through ports where ships docked, and people had no immunity to the new strain of the disease. Death often came a mere two days after the first flu symptoms appeared.

When scientists discover a new virus, they use devices called genetic sequencers to figure out what it is. Genetic sequencers show how similar a virus is to other viruses that have been previously discovered. When a new virus appears, scientists can use this information to guess its effects and how it will spread, because viruses similar to already-known viruses may behave in similar ways. Thanks to genetic sequencing, it is becoming easier to identify and track new viruses.

Organizations such as the WHO watch and respond to health threats around the globe. One way they attempt to contain diseases is through isolation. People exposed to an infectious disease may be quarantined, or kept in a hospital

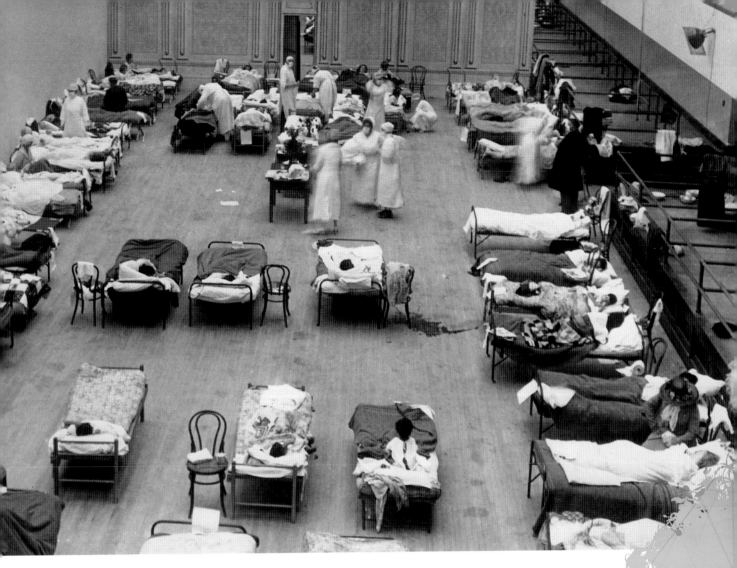

The 1918 flu pandemic left millions ill or dead.

apart from others. Even if they are not currently sick, they might become sick soon. Keeping them isolated stops a disease from spreading and becoming a pandemic.

PATIENT ZERO

Scientists trace the path of a virus backward to try to find the first human infected. This person is called patient zero. Patient zero is also called the index case. It is important to identify patient zero, because this patient can tell

People can wash their hands frequently and practice good hygiene to prevent the spread of diseases.

scientists how the virus first spread to humans, usually by identifying the natural reservoir that holds the disease between outbreaks in humans. It is often difficult to know if an individual is patient zero or merely an early victim of the disease.

HELPFUL STEPS

Meanwhile, people can take steps to protect themselves and the people they know from pandemics. If a person gets sick, he or she can stay home from work or school. People can visit the doctor and receive treatment. People who live near mosquitoes and other insects can avoid bites by wearing proper clothing or using insect repellent. Travelers can learn about the risk of disease in the destinations they visit, and everyone can be vaccinated whenever possible.

HOW SCIENCE WORKS
TRACKING VIRUSES

Nathan Wolfe is a virologist who is creating a pandemic early warning system. He founded Global Viral, an organization that promotes virus exploration and research. All around the world, scientists and staff members of Global Viral work together and share information. They try to spot viruses as soon as they appear.

Scientists collect and record blood samples from people with diseases, study diseased wild animals, and document the path of diseases. They pay careful attention to groups of people who are more likely than others to become infected with a new virus. Wolfe believes there is "nothing like on-the-ground information." His goal is to uncover and stop viruses before they can cause another pandemic.

FIVE

BEATING DISEASES

The idea of a future pandemic similar to the Black Death or the 1918 flu is scary. However, the scientific community has grown, too. Thanks to international research and sharing of information, it has become easier to prevent diseases from becoming widespread pandemics.

In the last century, science has won the battle against dozens of deadly diseases. Scientists have learned new ways to treat and prevent diseases that could become pandemics. Polio, typhus, measles, and rinderpest are just some of the infectious diseases scientists have learned to prevent by vaccination. Antibiotics can defeat many other diseases as well.

Polio vaccinations are distributed in Afghanistan.

SUPERBUGS

Doctors have used antibiotics to cure bacterial infections since the 1800s. But antibiotics do not always work, and some bacteria adapt to resist even the strongest antibiotics. The resulting drug-resistant bacteria are often called superbugs. Some of these superbugs can spread quickly. To combat the spread of superbugs, doctors take extra care to keep hospitals clean, and scientists also work to develop new kinds of antibiotics.

EBOLA OUTBREAK OF 2014

In late 2013, cases of the deadly Ebola virus began to appear in western African countries such as Guinea, Sierra Leone, and Liberia. Ebola virus can cause high fevers, rashes, and diarrhea. Some strains of Ebola have a mortality rate of 50 to 80 percent. By November 2014, more than 13,700 cases had been reported and more than half of those cases were fatal, though these numbers are likely underestimates because of poor reporting in developing nations.

Health and aid organizations took steps to prevent a pandemic. They isolated infected patients and taught communities how to recognize Ebola symptoms. Ebola

Amber Vinson was a nurse who contracted Ebola while caring for another patient in a Dallas hospital. She was declared Ebola-free on October 28, 2014.

can only be spread through direct contact with bodily fluids, such as blood. WHO and local governments took steps to prevent people with Ebola symptoms from leaving their countries and spreading the disease. Still, diseases like Ebola can take a heavy toll.

WHO'S GOALS

WHO and other organizations are working to develop a global tracking system for disease research and control.

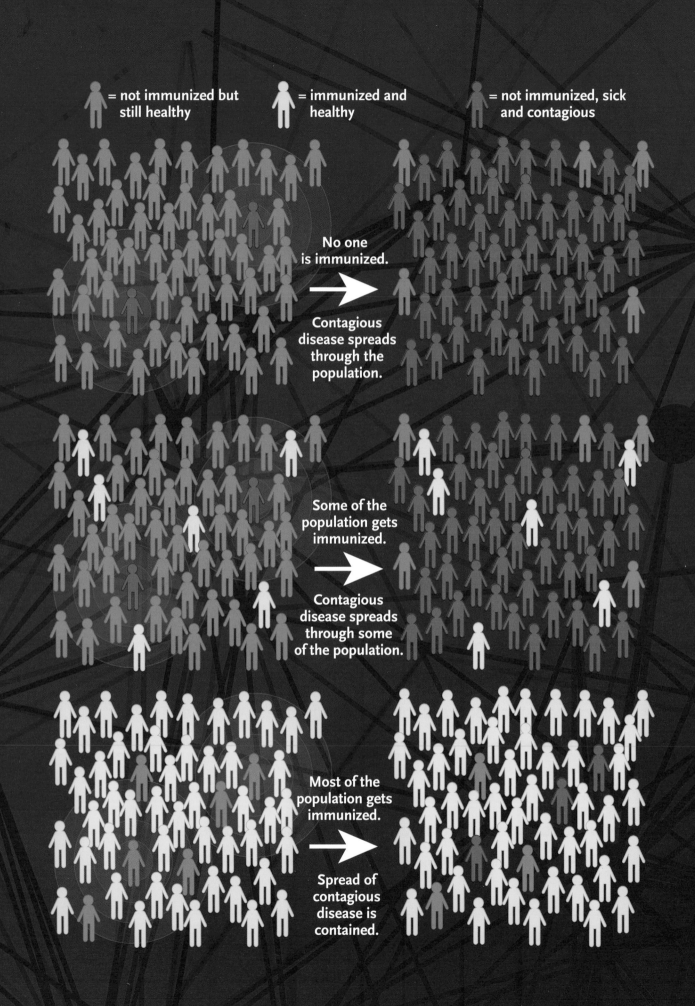

= not immunized but still healthy

= immunized and healthy

= not immunized, sick and contagious

No one is immunized. → Contagious disease spreads through the population.

Some of the population gets immunized. → Contagious disease spreads through some of the population.

Most of the population gets immunized. → Spread of contagious disease is contained.

HERD IMMUNITY

The diagram shows how herd immunity works. Using the diagram and the text from this chapter, explain herd immunity in your own words. Why is this idea so important in preventing pandemics?

They use computer databases to tell scientists around the world about local outbreaks. The Internet and social media are also being used to help track the spread of diseases.

WHO also aims to help developing nations prevent pandemics. Disease outbreaks are more common and harder to contain in developing nations because they lack the medical system to diagnose and prevent diseases early. Global efforts are needed to help poorer nations prevent the spread of diseases.

FLU SHOTS

Flu shots, which protect against the seasonal flu, are becoming more than just an option. They are required in some places, such as schools and hospitals. When enough people are immunized against a virus, together they form what is known as herd immunity. Once a certain percentage of people in a community are

PLEASE WASH
YOUR HANDS
BEFORE
ENTERING THE
SHOP

NOTICE

WHO works to provide poorer nations such as Sierra Leone with safe water supplies, better ways to deal with waste, and vaccination programs.

immunized, diseases have a much smaller chance of spreading and becoming pandemics.

Human beings have faced powerful microscopic enemies throughout history. These tiny killers have managed to survive, change, become resistant to drugs, and kill millions of people. But every day, science gets a step closer to winning the war against pandemics.

CASE STUDY

MODERN INFLUENZA

Robert G. Webster is a world authority on influenza. He and his research team study avian, or bird, flu strains in Southeast Asia. They track new strains of flu in different birds to watch for possible pandemics. They capture the birds, test their blood, and compare the different kinds of viruses they find.

The deadly flu virus H5N1 surfaced in 2004 among chickens and ducks from eight countries. In Thailand, Vietnam, Cambodia, and Indonesia, the virus also infected people. The H5N1 virus had changed to also survive inside human bodies. The scientists discovered the virus was also killing wild ducks and shorebirds. Since 2010, research teams have been working with Canadian wildlife officials to test migrating birds. Traveling birds could carry a deadly virus to new areas. Because some strains of these viruses can survive in people, scientists believe bird migration could lead to pandemics.

TOP TEN WORST
PANDEMICS

1. **SMALLPOX**

   Smallpox is a contagious virus that killed many American Indians. These deaths took place between the 1400s and 1800s. American Indians caught the disease from European settlers.

2. **TUBERCULOSIS**

   Tuberculosis is a bacterial disease that destroys the lungs. The disease has been discovered in Egyptian mummies, and ancient Greek authors wrote about its effects.

3. **THE BLACK DEATH**

   Also known as the bubonic plague, the Black Death is believed to be one of the first pandemics. It killed approximately one-third of Europe's population in the 1300s.

4. **TYPHUS**

   Typhus is a disease spread between humans by insects such as ticks, lice, and fleas. The disease is known for killing during wartime, when close and unsanitary living conditions among soldiers promote the spread of lice and other natural reservoirs.

5. YELLOW FEVER

Yellow fever is a deadly tropical disease spread by mosquitoes. There is no cure, but there is a vaccine against it. The disease still kills many where vaccines are not widely available.

6. MALARIA

There are records of malaria dating back more than 4,000 years. Mosquitoes spread the disease. Today there are more than 100 million of cases of malaria in sub-Saharan Africa alone.

7. HIV/AIDS

This sexually transmitted infection has killed approximately 36 million and infected nearly 75 million. Although there are medications to help manage the disease, there is no cure.

8. SPANISH INFLUENZA

A strain of influenza struck countries around the world in 1918 and 1919. Approximately 50 million people died.

9. MEASLES

Before a vaccine was invented and made widely available in the 1960s, 3 to 4 million cases of measles erupted in the United States each year.

10. CHOLERA

This bacterial disease has existed in India since ancient times. The rest of the world was exposed when trade grew between India and other countries. More than 100,000 people die each year from cholera.

GLOSSARY

ANTIBIOTICS: Drugs used to kill harmful bacteria and to cure infections.

CONTAGIOUS: Having a sickness that can be passed to someone else by touching.

CONTAMINATED: Infected by contact or association.

GENETIC SEQUENCERS: Equipment used to study the genetic code of a virus or organism.

HANTAVIRUS: Any RNA virus that infects specific rodents.

IMMUNE SYSTEM: The system that protects your body from diseases and infections.

INFECTIOUS: Capable of being passed to someone else by germs that enter the body.

MALARIA: A serious disease that causes chills and fever and is passed from one person to another by mosquitoes.

MICROBES: Germs.

PARASITES: Organisms living in, with, or on other organisms.

SANITATION: The promotion of hygiene and prevention of disease.

VECTORS: Living things that transmit diseases from one animal or plant to another.

ZOONOTIC: Diseases that can be spread from animals to humans.

FURTHER INFORMATION

BOOKS

Gardy, Jennifer. *It's Catching: The Infectious World of Germs and Microbes*. Berkeley, CA: Owlkids Books, 2014.

Marciniak, Kristin. *The Flu Pandemic of 1918*. Minneapolis: Abdo Publishing, 2014.

Piddock, Charles. *Outbreak: Science Seeks Safeguards for Global Health*. Washington, DC: National Geographic, 2008.

WEBSITES

http://kids.niehs.nih.gov/explore/hliving/pandemic_flu.htm
This website includes information about how to prevent the flu. It also tells how you can stay safe if a pandemic occurs.

http://medmyst.rice.edu
This interactive website features games that provide a fun and interesting way to learn about infectious diseases.

INDEX